Paint your wagon green

Initiatives in Marketing

CV Madhavi

Is going green innovation?

- Green is perched on the other side but inspire business innovation by ethics, opportunities, nature friendly business and buyer relationship building task completion of business convergence with market success without a single demarcation between customers and non Customer, profit and loss, products and alternative solutions.

Root driver

- Ofcourse desired Business goals and offerings are driven by Customer who is also driven by personal roots of trust and traditional values.
- Addressing roots will go with helping business changes and not the other way round.

Marketing is not money

- Budgeting is part of business activity but some people have to understand that Marketing is a common contextual place on inviting competitors and customers to understand the sales attributes (reps, product, price).

Green marketing

- Make a product look like a new window and miracle in customer life
- Advertisement is meant to exaggerate but retain natural drivers of Customer expectations when they are not pulled away from the offering otherwise don't ask Customer to give money.

Convertible green

- Change to green from red with your business disciplined for all departments' inclusion
- Try to make greener on fear in slipping into reds and pinks

Sales ferries

- If you sell something to buyer she is sure on parting with her money but not definite about your products so build trust by solving the latter.

Marketing Soccer

- Customer is not supposed to be a football but audience far off at judging the business rightly and informatively of business gimmick in marketing campaigns.

Ad Blitz

- Technology and decision sciences are two sides of ad strategy for win-win-win of Customer, company and competitors
- Competition as winner of strategic collaboration can grow innovative advertising.

Business bloom

- Businesses bring up topics based on dedicated cause and project from previous best or Customer worst as a dissatisfaction of Customer is door to new opportunities.

Betting knack

- Betting on sales and marketing is like expectations in ads showing pleasant dreams of Customer as company promise without fulfillment, so create product better than ad.

Gyration of advertising

- First ad is thought to be a good communication
- Then ad strategy is a good attempt of storytelling and celebrity gushing
- Next ad becomes mandatory competition
- Company is neither giving more nor best to customer

Sales and marketing rings

- High promotion stints and Customer rigging guide Customer to competitors because the more you are pushing your products the easier they are pulled to understand alternatives and buy competitors' products.

Promotion has pro

- It should be in favour of user and not bragging about the business offering
- The product should move from Business to customer but not as exaggeration on force

Channeling ideas

- Middle management of office and middlemen of supply chain can't be done away with so use the right resources like consumer references and Customer redeployment in vendor senior management to save expenses of confidentiality and brand.

Changing business values

- Ethics to ethical hacking
- Environment to green without human attachment
- Product superiority to network marketing
- Tomorrow's Customer to premium Customer

Value- need match

- The seller mentality needs to get even with total match to that of buyers
- Seller has to release all ego but respect buyers'
- Now what you give is a value for money and in line with consumer needs
- The business grounds are green for new products and ripening of Customer trust.

Designing corporate decision

- Systems vs brains of emotional sense of urgency so that we work with chaos, logic, clarity, usability, tips, context, experience, relevance but not flowchart and program that is ignorant of specificity of decision.

Mentoring taskforce

- The leader has to have a great follower team for guidance and learning from Customer in translation of Customer fraternity feedback to Business interpretation easy to be implemented by advanced technology teams to usability items and that four-way conversion need precision style detail-oriented mentorship.

Knowledge of utility of products

- Today is the time of users with information and access globally for Customer integration into business changes without complying with that knowledge while owning it, most manager teams know less than their customer.

Value Customer pick

- If you want a customer who searches for value it's better than others who will go with Customer of value Business as deal making profit
- A customer full of values can grow an appreciable firm with value for Customer by nurturing business of values

Gap in need and perceptions

- Often the perception of individuals is not in line with the accompanying needs of community and similarly the global economic goal may be at variance with local wars of business changes and development.
- Manage your problems by priority to social change.

Implementation vs impression

- Former is the child of latter
- First is employees responsibility, second is customer feedback engineered by company driven experience
- First you impress and execute, expectations are higher than when you complete the task and seek good impression

Improvement on reducing tats

- Green marketing is done by adapting to natural methods of promoting by silence, action in showing strong points of offering independent of spreading influence of competition in reducing tactics, artificial tags stating exaggerated product excellence.

New media marketing

- Stories from customers are better than data from systems
- Green marketing tells to understand Customer dreams into turning real and is done by ignoring statistics and numbers
- Avoid loss of natural resources in the process of marketing by using new media marketing tools.

Social sales

- Group buys from different states on globe will soon be real for bulk discount to volume scaling
- It will take care of payment security, information privacy, multilocular same size package and time delivery for equal Customer treatment on easy terms or none.

Technology ad-ing

- Digital art is creeping in seconds with ads by using the products and other business data
- Intelligent solutions show related ads by Customer search criteria on web
- Social networks could teach a lesson or preach on the usage.

Selling before marketing

- Old Customer testimonials and service delight feedback, form best channels for your business advertising, brand building and marketing by selling before marketing because they trust one another more than a ten seconds ad or demo or one free sample.

Sell products, buy culture

- Social networks work with interesting factors affecting business changes brought by Customer, unearth unexpected expectations and reset the business goals for selling new products after buying Customer cultures in inspiration.

Tasting ad trivia

- Green marketing wastes no resources, hi-but ads have to get out
- Put in common terms enacted by the users
- The best ad is to distribute one billion samples for saving five billion dollars in ads

Washing business changes

- More money goes without giving new productivity with customers from fragmented understanding, demand for the same thing from the different social networks.

Best business networking

- Build high values social networks between customers and employees to identify long term profitable opportunities because of more relevance than business hipower network with give-and-take business partnerships.

Ad-ditional social

- Hi-tech ventures and business innovation asking for Customer instead of own importance are utilising the social ad space in which Customer is the ad maker with her testimonials as advertisement to society without any testing or rework.

What to market

- The group and community gains of using your business products or services
- Gains in terms of special, general, experiential, knowledge, emotional and other forms of satisfaction
- Don't take up price for justification or other reason, if products are you (representatives of business), genuinely, buyer is at ease of paying any price.

Dependency on networks

- Expand Customer base with your understanding by their usage
- Experience and feedback become more than transparent with modern Customer acceptance by others as users
- Eradicate exploitation of fake employees to show as satisfied buyers.

Social networking and product

- A product that is sold is marketed well in business to be better off with social networks selling their products that are provided for reduced price in first purchase and further reduction depending upon the referral sales by old Customer.

Green marketing and services

- The by-product is not a big utility gadget but some application for your global health of community helped by business for shifting from one Customer to collective responsibility culture based on dedicated cause based interaction without creating pressure on resources and by providing environmental protection.

What is green media?

- Tested experience in managing more expectations in converting them to profitable economic development opportunities for innovative solutions for Customer importance without using any resources from the environment.

Green product

- Should not disturb their inner environmental protection
- Should not tamper with environment resources
- Should not use any of the links of the natural food chains
- The changes in the above direction are best way of Innovation.

Ultra green

- Hi-tech ventures as integration of business with community systems are supposed to have taken shape under backward environment preservation or future upliftment of environment by Customer friendly business initiatives to get new ultra green business innovation.

Green network is

- Communication with customers by building technology networks
- Avoid exhausting means of transport and resources to get personal interaction based interfacing
- Able to get multiple meetings at different points for same Customer at any time tuning in technology.

Drivers

- User emotions, sentiments, values and ethos
- Number of sub networks with each user
- Business interaction between nodes
- Value addition by each node
- Multiplicity in each node e.g. tree of one to five branches

Systematic network

- Start with a common need to get multiple new advocates and solicitors on your single Customer solution or other forms
- Add critical value of quality, feedback or corrections, to bring interaction with different representatives.
- Reward for multiplication of the business network members.

Synchronise with customers

- Don't thrash experience of Customer as emotional and try to get aligned with customers from start because anyway they could thrust their own expectations in forcing positive response from your support teams challenging to break bounds of business changes where rivals may struggle with competition.

Synergistic network

- First good from last node in network is related to synergy of products and services availed by previous nodes in customer gaining valuable time with business stakeholders present in the network free from hierarchical disorders and business weaknesses.

Synthesis in business

- Social networks could teach employees on communication to bring interaction acceptance by market or looking at decision from different directions to fulfill winning combination for new products that help customers achieve target in daily activities of routine.

Rendering network utility

- Mentoring users and buyer networks could begin a new step in building profitable opportunities for companies with innovation for Customer segments and community delight for Customer faith in business

Exclusive green

- Work with each customer to care exclusively because no customer can expect you to grow them by harming environment, this is true for each customer but not community of Customers who could come down by competition trying to satisfy their wants to overuse or damage environment

Social networks systems

- Specific guidance should be given to customer for service finding true instincts and culture of business with distinctive goals in increasing quality of Customer as smart solutions driver to understand in concurrence of other prospects in the network of dynamic online reality systems under maximum security for managing user data warehousing and analysis.

Gains in technology

- More technology is lucky to get the customer feel comfortable with security and employees to get multiple new issues sorted in the process of system dealings with the best technologies to reduce human errors in avoiding penalties under employee attitude.

Buyer against competitors

- When you seem to be taken as trusted and caring by Customer segment then competitors with intentions of dashing buyer hope against you are happy hiding your business success without a proper competitive advantage of value for Customer.

Nullified effect of Technologies

- Social networks could look into modern business promotion with a new perspective on knowledge shared in the interactions with customers to prove that its culture and fashion don't know if anything else will continue through technology beyond implementing thereby allowing nullification in customer satisfaction by service adding technology effects on outputs and not Customer interaction.

Trade green

- Use human networks but not systems for your business networking
- Don't depend upon the misguided tactics or exaggerated programs for new change management

Social is local

- The changes that need to work with the global business planning and community development have to be part of social networks but don't lose localisation due to lack of boundaries for online interaction

High end result

- Higher edges of green marketing and business networking could give customers prosperity by allowing network to play on informative topics for new type of Customer interaction with different companies viewing the best of suggestions that should avoid loss of change.

Marketing and greening

- Needs of Customer are simple but blamed for getting company work with environment to its chaos so greening of marketing campaigns by allowing reactions of cultural pursuits, not machine, total renewal of resources with no harm in environment and linking marketing effort to plantation of trees or other suitable initiatives.

Gating in the process

- Everything to help customers and business holds opportunities hidden by challenges of appeasing community to be in the best of growth and change phases, so Companies should make process rigorously exhaustive to account for new modes of development.

Eulogy in green innovation

- Product is manufactured by machine but thought by Customer and sold by employees, the need is to inform that technology is no indispensable so don't forego environmental protection for new technologies.

Media networking for

- Positioning and business changes with technology taking public opinion for your skill and task delegation or priority given by market or Customers with exchange at reactions or initiatives in community development.

Best efficiency

- Comes from social networks interaction based on usage improvement or product changes brought for risk management strategy by controlling competitors from disruptive innovation.

Technology

- Treating the Technology as giver of solutions can grow trained staff for handling tasks execution and Customer expectations in forcing out more challenging hiccups for further new business quest based on socially green methods.

Up trending social

- The changes that you want in community are propelled by relevant social reactions of networks marketing the same with products in adapting to natural methods winning on the fact and approval of majority, the company should hail their preference.

Best innovative network

- The changes are confidential yet may be driving trends in discussion on social networks with maximum Innovative competition in reducing the difference between stakeholders by providing common mission for winning smiles on Customers.

Remnants of network

- Partner feedback
- Expert comment
- Utility of products
- Preferences for technology
- Innovative needs

Strategy or social networks

- Strategic networks could bring out a good chain of deal management with maximum utilisation of capabilities and Strategies
- Social networks could teach you how to use machine for making products out of information from your non Customer groups building new ideas on improving their life.

Unprotected data and unproductive projects can grow more loss than profits leading to product rejection

Media is not green

- When we talk on representing the society but it's not too easy to accept and present opinion with the factual situations in real-time unless it's planned for losing the spontaneity
- Green media don't believe in showing facts but yielding value or perceptions change to form good opportunities for growth of Customer via business changes.

Networking for Customer

- New innovation is no different for exploring as exploiting the process and technology with Excellence in business unless they get multiple threads of Customer discussion on social networks.

> Network is like that need of Customer in common terms but specific condition

Build market power

- By inviting Customer as your quick response for competitive solutions in community connection by dropping differences of personal bias or exaggerated view because market power comes from Customer as smart driver of modern management network.

Plug n get benefits

- The product is on simple plug for getting benefits of social networks without any cost or conditions or efforts as such at run

Best value

- Participation and Customer as smart value of social networks could bring up success without a proper competitive strategy but for building new ideas.

Belonging network

- Social networks could look into future challenges that go into making or breaking or losing balance between customers and business representatives working with different development strategies in adjustments with their inconvenience of social gaps.

Beauty of technology

- Comes when social change comes from technology that could compare to end instead of amend your customer needs more on the commercial or other business interagency competition as indicators of network benefits.

Duty of business technology

- It's better to avoid technology than skip training the process owners and employees along with customers
- Product and services that provide utility within the boundaries of Customer expectations can be seen as duty of technology.

Similar pattern

- Outputs and methodology can grow you to stagnant industry if not managed better by players to get multiple transitions in balancing similarities and differences.

Awesome networks

- The social marketing and sales by Customer network collaboration can get you better market power of creation of innovative involvement of of Customer as smart driver of modern competition

Ok sorry

- The two sides of Technological independence and business changes could develop both solutions and results in favour of Customer as your quick response by paying agile response for supporting the collaborative ways or acceptance of business errors in ok and sorry.

Strategy for smart networks

We should not disseminate information on enhancing rivalry but business changes brought by Customer and accepted by business for cultivation of mutual benefits for next network participants including the existing ones.

Physiology of network

- Companies are the limbs, users are cells, ideas and discussion flow like energy, output resulting from your competitors and business can benefit the overall process of social marketing and economy participants of similarity like blood and water in replenishment of networks.

Media is a network

- Social media is the extension of networks beyond business groups in having multiple classes of business users, sponsors, partners and competitors for addressing Customer more correctly.

Expand Customer

- In user interface at different levels of business information management and interaction between the different stakeholders sinking for new change, the business mission fulfillment can get possible by expansion of Customer understanding for excellence of attaining the market improvement.

Rechristen network

- Rework, reward, reword that confusion of users of business products which can grow future opportunities to get new impact of social networking and marketing as community hives for passive products against active hives.

Collective bargaining of rut

- The user in business referral of convincing others who would not let you have any mood of Customer spoilt by advanced bargain tactics to eliminate competition, alternatives, price ruts or other issues could give good learning about bigger reason for collaborative global network.

Go with, Go with Customer of ..

- Check the need to be taken in accepting your business products by ignoring market and go with Customer needs and before competitors hunt for your user get the competitors behind by gathering need of their customer.

Squeezing

- Each social marketing effort is your favourite curry and Customer satisfaction tactic in offering differentiation and worth from the beginning itself in squeezing of business changes with distinct technology shifts.

Temporary networks

- Could give customers value without creating pressure of business products or experiments
- Are equally intelligent solutions for social marketing campaigns that are cost effective and business oriented.

Defy bounds

- It was limited to your immediate neighbours in business promotion with 1800s, today that would matter to distant nations how well your products are marketed on social marketing campaigns.

Logy of marketing

- Business is no longer depending upon marketing when Customer includes trust by your name
- Marketing is like yes of Customer forced by Companies.

Idea to marketing

- Marketing is done by companies struggling to hide their mistakes and winning competitor hides lies best
- A real sincere company should be doing minimum or no marketing.

Re-finding marketing

- Marketing is translation of business mistake to advertisement lies that are bought in product by Customer who rates rivals by the presentation on packaging of those weaknesses.

Real marketing

- Real marketing is company specialising for new products campaigning of Customer appreciation of their cultural importance or Customers themselves slowly improving excitement of business launches.

Real moon

- Marketing knack is not different from management of others product in the competitive dark clouds shining like a moon but they have observers for moonlit shadows cast by rival doubts.

Save buyers

- It's better for systematic benefits awareness introduction than trying into modern exaggeration of products that help with no value but profit by thrusting on Customer motivation of different baseless pointers.

Beginning to end

- Marketing is company internal journey brought outside by balancing business weaknesses, rival challenge and Customer demands because not one can be managed completely to perfection from the beginning of idea to end of product life.

Clean marketing

- Let Customer experience your business ideology from the inception of company but not as important message across marketing campaigns alone

No product ostentation

- The sincere effort and time invested in converting an opportunity to product should move forward from the process of product ostentation to customer partnership with involvement in getting ready for community acceptance.

Business values

- Marketing should not deter trust and integrity in customer
- Marketing should not disseminate information on loggerheads with business culture
- Marketing should be avoided in the interest of business value conservation.

Value of values

- Integrity as value of quality is fed back from Customer as trust
- Competitive selection of business products improving their values of global ethics serve as a common bond between provider -Customer.

Customer

- Is different in that they could create change or mess, use or ignore the message or product conveyed by marketing campaigns
- Uses product or technology services in meeting with needs before identifying with your marketing campaigns that are mostly ignored.

Best sellers

- Don't worry if the process and conditions of marketing are not followed in business
- Give top priority and favour on your customer preferences over global competitor responses for new marketing campaigns.

Use of marketing

- It will take step in favour of old Customer for giving new reason for buying your old products or new modification
- It inspires new customers at trying your Innovation as metoo or novel offering.

www.ingramcontent.com/pod-product-compliance
Lightning Source LLC
Chambersburg PA
CBHW020554220526
45463CB00006B/2302